Faith 4 LifE

SENIOR HIGH BIBLE STUDY SERIES

FAMILY MATTERS

Group

Loveland, Colorado

Group's R.E.A.L. Guarantee to you:

This Group resource incorporates our R.E.A.L. approach to ministry—one that encourages long-term retention and life transformation. It's ministry that's:

Relational

Because learner-to-learner interaction enhances learning and builds Christian friendships.

Experiential

Because what learners experience through discussion and action sticks with them up to 9 times longer than what they simply hear or read.

Applicable

Because the aim of Christian education is to equip learners to be both hearers and doers of God's Word.

Learner-based

Because learners understand and retain more when the learning process takes into consideration how they learn best.

SENIOR HIGH BIBLE STUDY SERIES

Family Matters

Visit our Web site: **www.grouppublishing.com**

Credits
Contributing Authors: John Cutshall, Mikal Keefer, Jane Vogel, and Jennifer Root Wilger
Editor: Amy Simpson
Creative Development Editor: Dave Thornton
Chief Creative Officer: Joani Schultz
Copy Editor: Lyndsay E. Gerwing
Art Director: Sharon Anderson
Print Production Artist: Stephen Beer
Cover Art Director/Designer: Jeff A. Storm
Cover Photographer: Daniel Treat
Production Manager: Dodie Tipton

ISBN 0-7644-2464-5

10 9 8 7 6 5 4 3 2 1   12 11 10 09 08 07 06 05 04 03

Printed in the United States of America.

FAMILY MATTERS

The family has never been more fragile than it is now, and today's teenagers are painfully aware of that. If they haven't directly experienced a divorce, they have friends who have. Changes in society are forcing redefinition of the concept of family on an ongoing basis. Today's young people need to learn about God's design for the family.

Teenagers need to know that God created marriage and the family and that he created them before anyone had sinned. God created family because he knew we couldn't bear to live alone. He created us to have spouses and children, brothers and sisters, and everyone else we call family. Family relationships should be characterized by mutual love and respect. When a family operates according to God's design, it can provide tremendous security, support, and growth.

When a family operates according to God's design, it can provide tremendous security, support, and growth.

In this book, teenagers will learn that their families are important to God. In the first study, they'll understand the purposes of family. They'll be encouraged that God can heal the hurts they've experienced and can help them pass along the blessings they've received.

In the second study, teenagers will explore how their actions affect their parents. As they try to see the relationship from their parents' point of view, they can discover that their parents need their respect and love.

In the third study, teenagers will discuss divorce and real love. They'll learn that God's love never fails, even in confusing and horrible circumstances.

The final study of this book will help teenagers understand some of the frustration they experience with their families. It will help students see that their desire for independence is a natural adolescent tendency. But it will also show them that they should be thankful for the safety and support they receive from their families and that they should strive to honor and respect their parents.

When your young people see and understand the guidelines God has given us for the family, they'll be better equipped to build and maintain positive family relationships that will benefit them for a lifetime.

SENIOR HIGH BIBLE STUDY SERIES

Faith 4 Life: Senior High Bible Study Series helps teenagers take a Bible-based approach to faith and life issues. Each book in the series contains these important elements:

• Life application of Bible truth

Faith 4 Life studies help teenagers understand what the Bible says and then apply that truth to their lives.

• A relevant topic

Each Faith 4 Life book focuses on one main topic, with four studies to give your students a thorough understanding of how the Bible relates to that topic. These topics were chosen by youth leaders as the ones most relevant for senior high students.

• One point

Each study makes one point, centering on that one theme to make sure students really understand the important truth it conveys. This point is stated upfront and throughout the study.

• Simplicity

The studies are easy to use. Each contains a "Before the Study" box that outlines any advance preparation required. Each study also contains a "Study at a Glance" chart so you can quickly and easily see what supplies you'll need and what each study will involve.

• Action and interaction

Each study relies on experiential learning to help students learn what God's Word has to say. Teenagers discuss and debrief their experiences in large groups, small groups, and individual reflection.

• Reproducible handouts

Faith 4 Life books include reproducible handouts for students. No need for student books!

• Tips, tips, and more tips

Faith 4 Life studies are full of "FYI" tips for the teacher, providing extra ideas, insights into young people, and hints for making the studies go smoothly.

• Flexibility

Faith 4 Life studies include optional activities and bonus activities. Use a study as it's written, or use these options to create the study that works best for your group.

• Follow-up ideas

At the end of each book, you'll find a section called "Changed 4 Life." This section provides ideas for following up with your students to make sure the studies stick with them.

Use Faith 4 Life studies to show your teenagers how the Bible is relevant to their lives. Help them see that God can invade every area of their lives and change them in ways they can only imagine. Encourage your students to go deeper into faith—faith that will sustain them for life! Faith 4 Life, forever!

FAMILIES IN INTENSIVE CARE

The robed minister led his congregation in the Lord's Prayer. "Our Friend, who art in heaven…" they droned together, heads bowed.

Huh? *"Friend"?*

"I no longer refer to God as 'Father,' " explained the minister later. "So many people have suffered pain in their families, and fathers are often not considered loving."

Fathers. Mothers. Brothers and sisters. The people who know us best have the power to bruise us most easily. A cutting word, a broken promise, or the simple lack of attention causes us pain that goes straight to the heart. Soon the offenses meld into an overwhelming list of grievances that weigh us down, hindering our ability to see eye to eye with our family members on anything.

Your young people experience family conflict, and as they seek more independence, these family differences intensify. But there's hope for healing, and this study will help your students discover where to find it.

THE POINT

God can heal your family's hurts.

SCRIPTURE SOURCE

Genesis 37:2-28
Joseph's brothers sell him into slavery.

Genesis 45:1-15
Joseph forgives his brothers.

THE STUDY AT A GLANCE

#1

For Starters

10 to 15 minutes

■ **SOCIAL HOUR**

What students will do:
Carry chairs while attempting to eat and drink refreshments.

SUPPLIES:
❑ cookies
❑ paper cups
❑ punch
❑ cassette or CD player
❑ cassette or CD
❑ folding chairs

#2

Bible Truth

30 to 35 minutes

■ **FAMILY WHEELS**

What students will do:
Diagram family communication for Joseph's family and their own families.

SUPPLIES:
❑ Bibles
❑ newsprint
❑ tape
❑ marker
❑ paper
❑ pencils

■ **OPTIONAL ACTIVITY**
30 to 35 minutes

What students will do:
Identify Joseph's family's hurts, how God healed those hurts, and how God can heal their own family's hurts.

SUPPLIES:
❑ Bibles
❑ napkins
❑ self-stick notes
❑ markers

#3

Life Application

5 to 10 minutes

■ **FORGIVE ME…
I FORGIVE…**

What students will do:
Ask God for forgiveness and pray to forgive family members.

As you discuss family hurts with your students, it's possible that a student may reveal that a parent or sibling has abused him or her. If this happens, you may have legal responsibilities to notify Child Protective Services or other agencies that will address the situation. To determine your legal duties as mandated in your state, contact the Child Help USA National Child Abuse Hotline at 1-800-422-4453.

Enlist adult volunteers to help you hand out chairs and monitor the activity.

Have a mop handy for potential spills. If you meet in a carpeted room, avoid serving drinks. Just serve snacks you can easily vacuum up!

BEFORE THE STUDY

Set out cookies and paper cups of punch. If possible, bring a cassette or CD player and some of your teenagers' favorite music to play during the "Social Hour" activity.

FOR STARTERS

10 to 15 minutes

SOCIAL HOUR

As teenagers arrive, play music if you brought some, and invite your students to eat, drink, and socialize. As each student picks up his or her refreshments, **ask** that person this question:

> **Have you ever been angry and held a grudge for at least a day?**

If that student says "yes," hand him or her a folding chair and explain that he or she must carry the chair for five minutes without letting it touch the floor. If any student allows his or her chair to touch the floor, hand that student another chair to carry in addition to the one he or she already has.

After five minutes, **ask:**

- **Did carrying your chair affect your ability to enjoy our socializing time? If so, how?**

- **Did carrying your chair affect your ability to relate to other people in the room? If so, how?**

- **How is carrying a chair throughout the room like carrying a grudge throughout life?**

Say: Carrying a chair during a party is similar to carrying a grudge against someone—they're both useless burdens that hinder us from fully enjoying what life has to offer. Yet while you probably wanted to let go of your chair in this activity, we often like to hold onto our grudges against others. When people hurt us, we find it difficult to forgive and forget. This is especially true in our families.

Today we'll look at a family that held grudges and see the pain that resulted from those grudges. We'll see how God healed that family's hurts and how God can heal your family's hurts.

BIBLE TRUTH

Want to help your teenagers increase communication in their families? Suggest that they take their family wheels home and, if they feel safe, explain their family wheels to their parents. Be sure to make this recommendation *after* the exercise has been completed so you don't discourage depth and honesty.

FAMILY WHEELS

Have teenagers form trios, and hand each trio a sheet of paper and a pencil. **Say:**

> We're going to examine Joseph's family. To do this, you're going to draw something called a "family wheel," which is a diagram that identifies the communication lines in a family. Let me show you an example.

Tape a sheet of newsprint to a wall, and draw the diagram illustrated in the margin. Or, if you wish, draw a family wheel that diagrams the communication lines of the family you grew up in.

If you use the example provided, **describe** it this way:

> In this family wheel, I'm in the middle because we're exploring how I relate to everyone else in my family. I communicate well with my dad, so I've drawn a straight line with arrows at both ends, signifying that the communication goes in both directions. My mom reaches out to me, but I don't often reciprocate, so I've drawn a straight line with an arrow pointed to me. On the other end of the line, I've drawn an X. My brother Scooter and I fight all the time, so I've drawn a zigzag line between us with arrows at both ends. And my dog Fido and I aren't communicating at all, so I've drawn a line with X's at both ends.

> Now that you've learned the finer points of creating family wheels, read Genesis 37:2-28 and, in your trios, create a family wheel that illustrates Joseph's family. Since we're examining how Joseph related to the rest of the family, draw the diagram with Joseph at the hub of the family wheel.

Ask: ● What were the hurts in Joseph's family?

● How did those hurts develop?

● Look at your trio's Joseph family wheel. What effect did those hurts have on the family?

● What responsibility did Joseph's brothers have for the family's hurts? What responsibility did Joseph have?

Hand a sheet of paper and a pencil to each student. Have students diagram their own families. Then have trios **discuss** these questions:

- What are your family's hurts?
- How did those hurts develop?
- Look at your own family wheel. What effect have those hurts had on your family?
- What responsibility does each of your family members, including yourself, have for those hurts?

Say: Joseph's brothers did a horrible thing to him when they sold him into slavery. Their action affected the whole family. But Joseph had his part too. He upset his brothers when he strutted around in his new coat and predicted that his brothers would bow down to him.

We all play a part in the hurts our families experience—parents, stepparents, siblings, stepsiblings, and us. But God can heal our family's hurts. Let's see ◄ THE POINT
how he healed Joseph's family.

Have trios read Genesis 45:1-15 and create new family wheels for Joseph's family based on what happened in the passage. When trios have finished, **ask:**

- What made this family transformation possible?
- How could God heal your family's hurts in a ◄ THE POINT
similar way?

Say: Joseph could have held a grudge against his brothers. In their time of need, Joseph could have let them suffer. Instead, he forgave his brothers for what they had done to him. And because he forgave them, God ◄ THE POINT
healed his family's hurts.

How could God heal your family's hurts through ◄ THE POINT
forgiveness? To answer that question, create a new family wheel that represents how forgiveness would affect your relationships with your family members.

When students have finished their new family wheels, have teenagers tell their trio members one thing they'll do in the coming week to begin to make their new family wheels a reality. For example, someone may choose to forgive a brother or sister for ruining a favorite clothing item. Then have teenagers tell each of their trio members how they know their trio members will succeed at their goals. For example, someone could say, "I know you'll succeed at asking your mom to forgive you because you have a lot of courage."

If you sense a high energy level within your group, use the following activity in place of the "Family Wheels" activity.

Hand each student a napkin (if possible, use yellow napkins). **Say:**

> **Being in a family can be a lot like playing football. There are hits and tackles, setbacks and advances. But football has an advantage: referees. When something unfair happens, referees throw their flags and blow their whistles. Then they turn to the stands, explain the foul, and proclaim a penalty for the offending team. Once that happens, it's over. The game goes on.**
>
> **Maybe your family could use a referee. Joseph's sure could have, and we're going to adopt that role. I'm going to read you the story of Joseph's family. As I do, listen for "family fouls"—the ways that Joseph's family members hurt each other. When you hear an "infraction," whistle and throw your "flag." We'll stop the "action," and then we'll attempt to learn from Joseph's and his brothers' mistakes.**

Before reading the story, have teenagers practice calling fouls by throwing their napkins and whistling. Then slowly read Genesis 37:2-28 aloud. Stop whenever someone throws a flag. Have whoever throws a flag explain the foul he or she noticed. Then write the infraction on a self-stick note, and stick the note to a wall. Once teenagers have fully discussed that foul, resume reading until someone else throws a flag.

After you've finished reading Joseph's story, you'll have a collection of self-stick notes on the wall. **Say:**

> **As we look at the infractions on this "wall of shame," we realize that Joseph's family needed major work to get beyond their hurts.**

Have each student turn to a partner to **discuss** these questions (encourage pairs to get up and look at the self-stick notes if they need to):

- **Do you relate to anything written on the self-stick notes? If so, what and why?**

- **What other family fouls have occurred in your family?**

- **What could Joseph or his brothers have done to make up for their family fouls?**

- **How can you help your family resolve issues that cause family fouls?**

- **How can God heal your family's hurts?** ◀**THE POINT**

When pairs have finished their discussions, **say:**

Let's see how God healed Joseph's family.

Have pairs read Genesis 45:1-15. **Say:**

Joseph had a prime opportunity in this passage. He could have evened the score in the game, making his brothers pay penalties for all the family fouls they'd committed against him. Joseph could have let his brothers go hungry or even imprisoned them. Instead he chose to forgive them, and because he did God healed his family's hurts. To represent this, let's remove all the notes from the wall. Have teenagers help you remove the self-stick notes, tear them up, and throw them away.

Hand each student a marker, and **say:**

This wall of shame is now clean. Think of what your family's wall of shame looks like right now. On your penalty flag, write a list of offenses and hurts that would appear on your family's wall of shame. You won't have to show this to anyone.

When teenagers have finished writing their lists, **say:**

Look at your lists. Remember that God healed Joseph's family's hurts when Joseph chose to forgive his family members.

Have teenagers turn to their partners to **discuss** these questions:

- **As you look at your list, how can God heal your family's hurts through forgiveness?**

- **Who do you need to forgive?**

- **Who do you need to ask to forgive you?**

- **What's one thing you'll do this week to help clear your family's wall of shame?**

Have each student tell his or her partner one quality the partner has that will help that person clear his or her family's wall of shame. For example, someone might say, "You're a good listener, and God will use your listening skills to heal your family's hurts."

Say: God can heal your family's hurts as you and your family members choose to forgive each other. Keep your penalty flag in a spot, such as a desk drawer or a journal, where it will remind you to seek forgiveness for those family fouls. As you forgive others and ask others to forgive you, mark off the situations that have been "cleared" from your family's wall of shame. When you've addressed all of the family fouls, destroy your penalty flag and throw it away.

LIFE APPLICATION

5 to 10 minutes

FORGIVE ME...I FORGIVE...

Dim the lights, and have each student find a place away from everyone else. **Say:**

> Get into a comfortable position. I'm going to lead us in a prayer time. In the Lord's Prayer, Jesus taught us to pray: "Forgive us our debts, as we also have forgiven our debtors" (Matthew 6:12). We're going to pray a similar prayer. I'll pray aloud, raising topics for us to discuss with God. After each topic, I'll pause for a few seconds to allow you to pray silently about that issue.

Pray: Dear God, we thank you that Jesus died to save us from the consequences of our sins. Right now, we confess all our sins to you. We confess to you those sins we've committed in our actions.

Pause for fifteen seconds, then **pray:**

> We confess those sins we've committed in our attitudes.

Pause for fifteen seconds, then **pray:**

> We confess sins we've committed in our secret thought life.

Pause for fifteen seconds, then **pray:**

> And we confess sins of not doing what you've called us to do.

Pause for fifteen seconds, then **pray:**

> We don't deserve your forgiveness. We've done nothing to earn it, but we ask for you to forgive us our part in putting your Son to death on the cross.

Pause for fifteen seconds, then **pray:**

> We also ask you to forgive us for our part in our families' hurts.

Pause for fifteen seconds, then **pray:**

> Thank you, Father. We feel the weight of our sin lifting as you bring us freedom.

> Now, Lord, we ask for your grace to flow through us to our families. We ask you to help us forgive those who have hurt us by accident, intent, or neglect.

*FYI

God's forgiveness makes it possible for our families to heal from the hurts we inflict on one another. To further empower your students to implement healing in their families, encourage them to study the following Bible passages:

● Psalm 130:3-4, 7-8— God forgives us for our sins.

● Matthew 18:21-22— Jesus says that we must forgive people seventy-seven times.

● Mark 2:1-12—Jesus forgave a paralyzed man and then healed him.

● Luke 19:1-9—Jesus forgave Zacchaeus.

● John 21:15-19—Jesus symbolically forgave Peter for denying him.

● Acts 2:38-39—Peter proclaimed the forgiveness of sins through Jesus' death and resurrection.

Pause for fifteen seconds, then **pray:**

Help us show your love to others, Lord.

Pause for fifteen seconds, then **pray:**

We pray in the name of Jesus, amen.

Many family counselors view families as systems—groupings of unique and important people who unite to create a whole and original entity. Just as a car is a system with each part relying on the others to make the car run, each family member's behavior affects how everyone else acts to make the family function (or dysfunction). For example, if Elizabeth yells at her mom, her mom might yell back, her stepbrother might withdraw, and her stepdad might attempt to mediate the conflict.

According to family systems theory, when one family member changes how he or she usually acts in certain situations, the system reacts in one of two ways: It attempts to squelch the changes in that one person to maintain the accustomed balance, or it changes to achieve a new way of interacting. For example, if Elizabeth usually yells at her mom but instead chooses to walk away from the conflict, her mom might either yell at her to encourage Elizabeth's usual reaction or her mom might give Elizabeth some space and then calmly approach her later.

This systems view partly explains why families with adolescents experience so much chaos. As your young people mature and desire more independence, the rest of the family has to adjust. Some family members don't want to adjust; they'd rather that things remain as always. Others want to accommodate the changes but don't know how. In addition, most families with adolescents must also accommodate parents in midlife, also a tough life passage. These forces combine to push even the healthiest family out of balance.

Understanding family systems helps you, your young people, and your young people's parents navigate through these tumultuous times. This understanding may help families realize that they're going to step on each other's toes from time to time. It doesn't make the struggles any easier, but at least families can realize that they're just like every other family with adolescents.

Family systems theory can also help your young people understand how God can use them to heal their families' hurts. As teenagers react differently to the people they live with, everyone else must change. As your young people offer forgiveness instead of anger to parents, stepparents, siblings, and stepsiblings, these family members can also change their behavior. The positive change of one person forgiving another can help families out of deep, dark holes of discouragement, despair, bitterness, and frustration.

HASSLE-FREE HOME

"**C**an you drop me off at Shana's? We're going to a movie, so I'll need some money. Oh, and we'll be back late, so don't wait up. I'll call if I need a ride."

Many teenagers treat their parents like the drive-through window at McDonald's. They don't stop to talk. There's no time. They just "drive up," order what they need, and move on. Parents aren't people; they're providers, cooks, maids, police officers, and chauffeurs.

Is this what *family* is supposed to be?

This study helps teenagers look at their families in a new way by exploring what their parents need and by discovering creative ways young people can serve the ones who love them most.

THE POINT

Your parents need your respect and love.

SCRIPTURE SOURCE

Ruth 1:1-22; 3:1–4:15
Ruth shows extraordinary love and loyalty toward her mother-in-law, Naomi, while Orpah does not.

1 John 3:18; 5:1-2
John teaches that we show love for God when we love others.

THE STUDY AT A GLANCE

#1

For Starters
10 to 15 minutes

■ **PARENT TALES**

What students will do:
Answer questions about their relationships with their parents.

SUPPLIES:
❑ slips of paper
❑ marker
❑ tape

■ **OPTIONAL ACTIVITY**
10 to 15 minutes

What students will do:
Act as parents trying to solicit information from their teenagers.

#2

Bible Truth
15 to 20 minutes

■ **ORPAH'S EXCUSES**

What students will do:
Compare Orpah and Naomi's relationship to their relationships with their parents.

SUPPLIES:
❑ Bibles
❑ paper
❑ pencils
❑ magazines
❑ modeling clay
❑ scissors
❑ construction paper
❑ markers

#3

Life Application
20 to 25 minutes

■ **LEGACY OF FAITH**

What students will do:
Discover that the strength of Ruth and Naomi's relationship was a shared faith and then write letters to their parents.

SUPPLIES:
❑ Bibles
❑ newsprint
❑ markers
❑ tape
❑ pens or pencils
❑ paper

■ **BONUS ACTIVITY**
5 to 10 minutes

What students will do:
Gather candy "grain" to represent ways they'll show love to their parents.

SUPPLIES:
❑ Bible
❑ bag of individually wrapped candies

If you don't have chairs in your meeting area, tape the slips of paper along the baseboards or in another inconspicuous place. After you introduce the activity, tell teenagers where to find their questions.

Every teen-parent relationship is different. Teenagers may view their parents as their best friends, worst enemies, or anything in between. Some teenagers live with both parents, some with single parents, and some with stepparents. In a perfect world, all parents would be understanding friends and positive role models for their teenage children. However, many parents today have "checked out" of their teenagers' lives. They express disapproval of their teenagers' attitudes and actions without taking time to understand them.

As you lead this study, avoid making generalizations about teenagers' parents. Instead, help teenagers examine their relationships with their parents so they can understand why their parents act the way they do. Encourage teenagers to offer respect and love to their parents out of love for God, even if they feel that their parents don't deserve it.

BEFORE THE STUDY

For the "Parent Tales" activity, write each of the following questions on a separate slip of paper. Make enough slips of paper for everyone to have one. It's OK to repeat questions. Tape the completed slips of paper underneath teenagers' chairs. Make sure adjacent chairs have different questions taped to them. Here are the questions:

● Where's one place you wouldn't be caught dead with your parents?

● What's one thing your parents do that drives you crazy?

● When have you been embarrassed by your parents?

● What's the most fun you've had with your parents?

● When have you been proud of your parents?

FOR STARTERS

10 to 15 minutes

PARENT TALES

After teenagers arrive, **say:**

> **Today we're going to explore our relationships with our parents. Some of us have two parents; some have one parent. Some of us have great parents; some have parents we think aren't so great. Like it or not, our relationships with our parents are lifelong. Let's start out by sharing some experiences we've had with our parents.**

Have teenagers remove the papers from under their chairs and discuss the questions with partners. After teenagers have discussed the questions, **say:**

> **Now turn your questions around and answer your questions from your parents' point of view. For example, if your question was, "When have you been embarrassed by your parents?" you'll now discuss, "When have your parents been embarrassed by you?"**

After pairs have discussed their questions, **say:**

> **Relationships with parents go both ways. You and your parents will have times you're glad to be related and times you wish you'd never laid eyes on each other. But in order for your relationships to thrive, you need to understand that your parents need your respect and love. Let's find out about the relationship between a parent and two daughters-in-law in the Bible.**

◀ THE POINT

OPTIONAL ACTIVITY

You may want to try this optional activity in place of the "Parent Tales" activity.

Have teenagers form pairs. Assign one student in each pair to be the parent and one student to be the teenager. **Say:**

> **How many of you have parents who ask you how your day went? You come home at the end of the day, and you're greeted by "How was your day?" Let's step into that situation for a few minutes.**
>
> **Parents, I'd like you to ask your teenagers about their day. Your goal is to find out what happened. Teenagers, I'd like you to think about everything that happened yesterday. You must answer all of your parents' questions honestly but as vaguely as possible. Your goal is to keep your parent in the dark. After a few minutes, you'll switch roles.**

If some teenagers happened to spend all day yesterday with their parents, have them simply think about another day when they weren't with their parents.

Allow a few minutes for parents to question their teenagers, then have teenagers switch roles. After teenagers complete the activity, **say:**

> **OK, let's see what it's like to be a parent.**

Ask: ● **As a parent, what did you learn about your teenager's day?**

Invite several teenagers to share, then **ask:**

> ● **As a teenager, were you able to keep your parent in the dark? Why or why not?**

Invite teenagers to fill in any missing details for their parents, then have pairs **discuss** the following questions:

> ● **What was it like to try to get information from your partner?**
>
> ● **What was it like to try to keep information from your partner?**
>
> ● **How was this activity like or unlike the way you communicate with your parents?**

- How do you know whether your parents are interested in your daily activities?

- Do you think your parents want to know what's going on in your life? Why or why not?

Say: It's easy for teenagers and parents to become foreigners to each other—you live your life and let your parents live theirs. It takes time and effort to create the common ground that fosters good relationships with parents. **Your parents need your respect and love.** You can show love to your parents by letting them into your life. Who you hang out with, where you go, what you do after school—sharing the events of your day can help parents feel like they're part of your world. Let's find out about the relationship between a parent and two daughters-in-law in the Bible.

BIBLE TRUTH

15 to 20 minutes

ORPAH'S EXCUSES

Have teenagers stay in their pairs and once again assume the roles of parent and teenager. Distribute paper and pencils. **Say:**

> We're going to explore the parent-child relationship between Naomi and her two daughters-in-law, Ruth and Orpah. Naomi was an older woman, and after her husband and sons had died, she planned to leave her daughters-in-law and return to her home country. We'll read her story in the Bible to find out how both daughters-in-law responded. Set out magazines, modeling clay, scissors, construction paper, and markers.

> Parents, you're each Naomi. Read Ruth 1:1-22; 3:1–4:15. Based on what you read, work alone to create something to represent Naomi. You can use any supplies you find in the room. For example, you could create a collage of images that tell us something about Naomi's personality, or you could create a life-size model of how you think Naomi looked.

> Teenagers, you're each Orpah. As you read Ruth 1:1-22; 3:1–4:15, you'll discover that Orpah chose not to go with Naomi. Based on what you read, work alone to make a list of excuses for why you'd choose not to go. Put your real name at the top of your list.

After teenagers have completed their assignments, call everyone back together. Invite each Naomi to describe his or her creation. Then collect the lists of excuses from the Orpahs. **Say:**

> Naomis, stay with your creations. Orpahs, stand next to your partners' creations.

Wait for teenagers to rejoin their partners. Then **continue:**

> Orpahs, as I read these lists of excuses, I'd like you to dismantle your Naomis' creations. Each time I read one of the excuses, remove a piece of your partners' creations.

Read the excuses, one at a time. Continue reading excuses until all the creations are destroyed. Then have teenagers **discuss** the following questions in pairs.

> ● Naomis, what were you thinking as your creations were dismantled?

If teenagers need help completing their Naomi assignments, encourage them to focus on a specific characteristic of Naomi, such as old age, sadness, or widowhood.

If teenagers need help completing their Orpah assignments, encourage them to have fun compiling their lists. Suggest excuses such as "I have to tend my husband's grave" or "If I walk that far, my shoes will wear out, and I won't be able to afford new ones."

- Orpahs, how did you feel as you dismantled the creations?

- How is Naomi and Orpah's relationship like or unlike your relationship with your parents?

- In this activity, the Orpahs' excuses hurt the Naomis' creations. When have you said or done things that hurt your parents?

Say: While it was fun for the Orpahs to come up with excuses, they didn't realize that their excuses would destroy the Naomis' creations. Sometimes we get so wrapped up in our own lives that we don't realize how our words or actions affect our parents. It's easy to forget that parents are people with feelings too. Your **THE POINT** parents need your respect and love. Let's see what we can learn about love and respect from Ruth's relationship with Naomi.

LIFE APPLICATION

20 to 25 minutes

LEGACY OF FAITH

Have teenagers number off from one to four, then have the ones, twos, threes, and fours gather in separate areas of the room. Give each group a sheet of newsprint and a marker.

Ask a volunteer to read Ruth 1:16-17 aloud. **Say:**

> Out of love, Ruth made a promise to stay with Naomi as long as she lived. Our relationships with our parents are lifelong too. In your groups, use the parts of Ruth's promise to brainstorm ways you can improve your relationship with your parents. List your ideas on the newsprint I gave you.
>
> Ones, focus on "Where you go I will go." Brainstorm places you can go or things you can do with your parents.
>
> Twos, focus on "Where you stay I will stay." Brainstorm ideas that can help you and your parents get along at home.
>
> Threes, focus on "Your people will be my people." Brainstorm ways you and your parents can accept and encourage each other's friendships.
>
> Fours, focus on "Your God [will be] my God." Brainstorm ways you and your parents can support each other's faith.

Allow time for teenagers to record their ideas, then post each group's newsprint on a wall. Have teenagers form foursomes to discuss their ideas. Make sure foursomes include one person from each group.

After teenagers have finished their discussions, call everyone back together and distribute paper and pens or pencils. **Say:**

> Ruth and Naomi's relationship flourished because they shared a common faith. Our faith can help us build stronger relationships with our parents, too. Your parents need your respect and love. Your love for God can help you love your parents, even when they seem unlovable.
>
> Take a few minutes alone right now to focus on your relationship with your parents. Think about what's

FYI

To help teenagers discuss their ideas, suggest that teenagers choose three of their favorite ideas from the various lists. Have teenagers tell why they think those ideas would work well in their families.

You may want to type the teenagers' ideas later and distribute them to teenagers or their parents.

 THE POINT

good in the relationship and what's not so good. Think about what you need from and what you can offer to your parents spiritually and emotionally. Then write a letter to your parents that expresses your thoughts. Don't sign your name. After today's meeting, I'll type the letters and post them anonymously where parents will see them.

Allow a few minutes for teenagers to write their letters, then call everyone back together. Collect the letters, and have teenagers form a circle. **Say:**

It's not always easy to maintain relationships with our parents. Before we close, let's take time to pray for those relationships. Pray silently for the person on your right. After a few moments, I'll close.

Allow a few moments for teenagers to pray, then close with a brief prayer asking God to help teenagers offer respect and love to their parents.

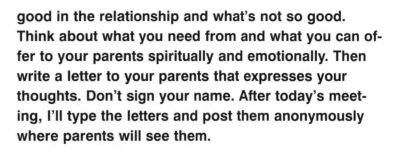

When Ruth chose to go with Naomi, her actions were contrary to cultural expectations. Ruth was a Moabite, and Moabites and Israelites were longtime enemies. According to Deuteronomy 23:3-6, Moabites weren't permitted to worship with Israelites; and Israelites were forbidden to wish for the Moabites' peace or success. In spite of this negative history, Ruth and Naomi managed to sustain a loving relationship. Ruth reached out to accept Naomi's faith in the one true God, and Naomi sent Ruth to Boaz to ensure Ruth's welfare.

Like Ruth and Naomi, teenagers and parents who pursue strong, healthy relationships may find themselves exceptions in a culture filled with broken and dysfunctional families. Use Ruth's example to encourage teenagers that the time and energy they invest in their parents will produce loving, lifelong friendships.

 **BONUS ACTIVITY**

If you have time, try this fun, feel-good extra activity.

Say: **After Ruth and Naomi arrived in Bethlehem, Ruth continued to show love for Naomi by going to the fields and gathering grain for food. We don't have to gather grain as Ruth did, but we can show love for our parents in other ways.**

Empty a bag of individually wrapped candies onto the floor. Have a volunteer read 1 John 3:18; 5:1-2 aloud, then **say:**

First John 3:18 says, "Let us not love with words or tongue but with actions and in truth." Gather one candy "grain," and give it to someone. As you give away the candy, point out a caring action you've seen that person do. Then tell the person one caring action you'll do for your parents this week. Gather a second candy grain to remind you to do it.

Allow time for teenagers to gather their candies, then call everyone back together. **Say:**

Your parents need your respect and love. **Your relationship** **with your parents may sometimes get rocky, but with respect and love, it will endure.**

Society often casts parent-teen relationships in a negative light. Movies, the media, and popular culture portray a constant struggle between teenagers and parents. But the reality may not be as bleak as it seems. In preparation for this study, we surveyed more than eighty average churchgoing teenagers about their interactions with their parents and got these results:

● 87 percent agreed with the statement "My parents respect me."
● 76 percent agreed with the statement "I respect my parents' point of view."
● 76 percent spend at least half an hour talking to their parents each day.
● 61 percent spend time doing things with their parents at least twice a week.

WHEN THE VOW BREAKS

Children of divorce have a hard time in life. Compared to teenagers who don't come from divorced families, these teenagers are likelier to drop out of high school, struggle getting a job, or become teenage parents.

They live in a society in which marriage is a disposable commitment, and the fallout from their parents' choice plagues them with questions that won't go away: "Is anything in life unshakable?" "Will the ones I love always leave me?" "Is there anyone I can really depend on?"

Of course you know the answer. Do your young people?

This study takes teenagers on a trip through the Promised Land to demonstrate how God's love can never fail them even when those they love most walk away.

THE POINT

God's love never fails you.

SCRIPTURE SOURCE

Joshua 1:1-9
God promises never to leave or abandon Joshua.

THE STUDY AT A GLANCE

#1

For Starters

20 to 25 minutes

■ **TOPOGRAPHERS 'R' US**

What students will do:
Form teams to construct a room-size topographical map of the land of Canaan.

SUPPLIES:
❏ Bibles
❏ masking tape
❏ scissors
❏ paper
❏ markers
❏ assorted craft supplies
❏ "This Land Is Your Land—Promise!" handouts (p. 37)

#2

Bible Truth

20 to 25 minutes

■ **CLAIMING THE PROMISED LAND**

What students will do:
Trace Joshua's journey and explore how God kept his promise to Joshua.

SUPPLIES:
❏ Bibles
❏ "This Land Is Your Land—Promise!" handouts (p. 37)

#3

Life Application

5 to 10 minutes

■ **STANDING ON THE PROMISED LAND**

What students will do:
Stand on the map at the landmarks that represent where they are in their family lives now.

SUPPLIES:
❏ "This Land Is Your Land—Promise!" handouts (p. 37)
❏ newsprint
❏ marker
❏ tape

■ **BONUS ACTIVITY**
up to 5 minutes

What students will do:
Discuss the impact of discovering that God makes the same promise to them as he did to Joshua.

SUPPLIES:
❏ Bibles

BEFORE THE STUDY

In this study, teams of three will transform your meeting room into a topographical map of the Promised Land, using the handout "This Land Is Your Land—Promise!" Estimate how many teams of three you expect to form, and photocopy enough handouts so that each person can have one.

Also, create the seven regions marked on your map by laying lines of masking tape on your meeting-room floor. That will help teenagers transfer the information from the handout onto the classroom floor more easily.

Next, choose which supplies you'd like to provide for the transformation process. You can make this project as simple or as elaborate as you wish, depending on what you provide. Here are some ideas for useful supplies; choose as many or as few as you wish and add your own creative ideas:

- brown paper bags or newsprint (teenagers can use these to cover chairs to make mountains, draw pictures, create flat desert lands, and so on);
- stones (for altars, rocky areas, hills);
- colored construction paper;
- aluminum foil (fun for water);
- wood blocks, bricks, or cardboard blocks (especially fun for the tumbled walls of Jericho); and
- mothballs (for the hailstones that fell on Gibeon).

FOR STARTERS

20 to 25 minutes

TOPOGRAPHERS 'R' US

As teenagers arrive, form "topography teams" of three. Give each person a photocopy of "This Land Is Your Land—Promise!" (p. 37). (Tell teenagers to keep track of their handouts; they'll use them again later on.) Assign each team one region of the map and a corresponding section of the meeting room to turn into a three-dimensional topographical map using the supplies you've provided. Let teenagers know that, later in the study, they'll be leading tours of their areas, so they should look up any unfamiliar episodes listed for their regions from the handout now and be prepared to tell what happened.

While teenagers work, go around the room and ask teams to explain what part of the land they're creating and how it relates to Joshua's life. If teenagers aren't familiar with Joshua's story, take this opportunity to familiarize them with the stories they'll be studying in detail later.

Don't worry about your group's size being too small or too large to do this activity. If you have fewer than twenty-one teenagers, assign some groups more than one region to create. If you have more than twenty-one teenagers, give more than one group the same region to transform, and have the groups work together.

BIBLE TRUTH

20 to 25 minutes

CLAIMING THE PROMISED LAND

When all the teams have finished with their regions, gather at the starting point (see the handout) on the bank of the Jordan River. Distribute Bibles, then **say:**

> Today we're going to talk about divorce and explore how it affects the way we live. To do that, we're going to go on an exploration of a very old land—the "Promised Land" you've created here.

Have teenagers open their Bibles to Joshua 1:1-9. Then **say:**

> I'm going to read aloud Joshua 1:1-9. This episode takes place after Moses had led the people of Israel out of slavery in Egypt and after he had led them through the wilderness for forty years. Moses had been a very important person to the people of Israel.

Read the passage aloud while teenagers follow along in their Bibles. Then **ask:**

- If you'd been Joshua, how would you have felt about losing your hero and leader, Moses?

- In what ways might it have seemed that Moses and maybe even God had failed Joshua?

- Why did Joshua need to be strong and courageous?

- If you had been Joshua, would you have believed all the promises God was making here? Why or why not?

- How are the feelings you have when your parents (or a friend's parents) get divorced like the feelings Joshua had when Moses died?

- In what ways does it seem like parents and maybe even God have failed you when your parents break up?

- When you're coping with divorce, what challenges do you face that require strength and courage?

- In rough times like that, how easy is it for you to believe God's promise that God's love never fails you?

Say: Let's follow Joshua's route and see whether God kept his promises to Joshua. As a group, walk along the

FYI

If many of your students have not struggled with divorce in their own families or a family close to them, you can broaden this topic by asking teenagers to reflect on any ways they've felt abandoned.

route Joshua took as shown on the handout. Stop at each landmark, and have a member of that region's team explain what happened.

At each stop, have teenagers find a partner and **discuss** these questions:

- What circumstances in this situation required strength and courage?

- How did God demonstrate that he was with Joshua in this situation?

- How do you think this experience influenced Joshua's understanding that God's love never fails?

When you reach the journey's end at the hills of Debir, read aloud Joshua 11:23b from the handout: "Then the land had rest from war."

Have teenagers turn to their partners and **discuss** these questions:

- How do you think Joshua felt spending all that time in war?

- How is coping with divorce like being in a war?

- How does knowing that God's love never fails you help you be strong and brave, even if your parents divorce?

*FYI

If you have more than twenty students, or your meeting room is small, you may prefer not to have all the teenagers explore the Promised Land as one group. As an option, you can form three groups by having members of each topography team number off, then cluster with other teenagers according to their assigned numbers. Assign each group an adult volunteer, then have groups follow each other through the exploration of the topographical map.

LIFE APPLICATION

5 to 10 minutes

STANDING ON THE PROMISED LAND

Say: **Look again at the map. Choose the spot that best represents where you are in your family life right now. For example, you might choose the bank of the Jordan River because your family is facing a difficult obstacle that will take God's special help to overcome. Or you might choose a site of a battle if you feel like your family is always fighting or the hills of Debir if your family is having peace after some bad fights.**

Encourage teenagers to look at the map on the handout to remember what all the landmarks are. Then **say:**

Once you've chosen the spot that best represents where you are, go stand there on our room map. When everyone is standing at a spot on the map, **say:**

Now turn to the person closest to you on the map and share how your spot on the map represents your life right now.

After teenagers share, **say:**

Now take turns praying for each other. When you pray, pray about these three things:

- **Ask God to give your partner strength and courage to face the challenges coming up,**

- **praise God for a specific way your partner has shown courage in facing challenges in family life, and**

- **thank God that his love never fails you.** ◀THE POINT

Write the prayer instructions on newsprint, and tape it to the wall. Then have teenagers pray together. After the prayer, **say:**

Choose an item from the map near you to take home with you. Place it next to your bed all this week as a reminder that, no matter what happens in your family, God's love never ◀THE POINT **fails you.**

If you have time and you want to continue the discussion, try this activity.

Have teenagers get back in their original topography teams of three. Make sure everyone has a Bible.

Say: **In your threesome, have each person read aloud one verse from Hebrews 13:4-6, then discuss these questions:**

● **What would you say to someone who told you that God's promise to be with Joshua doesn't apply to us today?**

● **What have you learned from Joshua's experiences that can help you cope with the divorce of people you care about?**

"If you were divorced, you wouldn't fight. I wish you were divorced," wrote one young person in a therapy group for children whose parents had filed for divorce.

Some teenagers are glad when their parents divorce, particularly when physical abuse or substance abuse has been a problem. These teenagers may not grieve for the absent parent or wish their parents were back together, but they share the feelings of abandonment and betrayal that other children of divorce experience. For these teenagers, the sense of loss is not that a once-happy family has been broken apart but that they never had a happy family.

So when teenagers tell you they're glad their parents divorced, ask them to describe their *ideal* family and discuss how that differs from their real-life experience. This will help teenagers begin to recognize and work through the hurts caused by their parents' divorces.

Today's teenagers have grown up in an era in which about one out of every two marriages ends in divorce. But the fact that divorce is so common doesn't make it any less painful. Judith Wallerstein, a clinical psychologist who studied 131 children of divorce for a span of fifteen years, "found them to be at higher risk for depression, poor grades, substance abuse, and intimacy problems."

Even if the teenagers you know don't seem to have those problems, don't assume they've dealt with their parents' divorces and moved on. Wallerstein says that when she did follow-up studies on teenagers eighteen months after their parents' divorces, "We didn't see a single child to whom divorce was not the central event of their lives."

How do you teach about God's love from a violent, war-filled book such as Joshua? What will you say when your students ask, "How could a loving God demand so much bloodshed?"

To understand the book of Joshua, we have to see how it fits into the big picture of God's relationship with his beloved people, Israel. With all the world around them refusing to acknowledge the true God, God consistently warned the Israelites not to be lured away from him to join in the worship of pagan gods. But because God knew how likely the Israelites were to be influenced by their pagan neighbors, he commanded them to drive out or destroy all sources of temptation to idolatry.

The war Israel waged on the Canaanites was more than a conquest for the land that had been promised to Abraham. It was evidence of God's desire to preserve Israel's purity in a loving relationship with God—rather than allow them to destroy themselves by worshipping false idols.

Despite this, your teenagers may argue, "But was it necessary to kill everyone, including babies and young children?" Future events showed that it was. God knew those people that Israel did not destroy would rise up in the future and become a terrible danger to Israel's faith and well-being. The book of Judges details the sad history of Israel's spiritual and physical downfall at the hands of people they failed to drive out of Canaan.

How does all this relate to your students today? The book of Joshua makes it clear that it was God, not the army, who fought the battles for Israel. When your students face the spiritual and emotional battles of coping with divorce, they can count on the unfailing love of God, who fights to keep his children free and close to his heart.

THIS LAND IS YOUR LAND—
PROMISE!

1. Jordan River: God parted the river so the people could walk through on dry ground *(Joshua 3)*.

2. Joshua built an altar to commemorate how God dried up the river *(Joshua 4)*.

3. Jericho: The walls came a'tumbling down *(Joshua 6)*.

4. Ai: The Israelites burned this enemy city to the ground *(Joshua 8:1-29)*.

5. Mount Ebal: Joshua and the Israelites built an altar and renewed their commitment to God *(Joshua 8:30-35)*.

6. Gibeon: God sent hailstones to defeat the enemy and made the sun stand still *(Joshua 10:1-15)*.

7. Hills of Debir: "Then the land had rest from war" *(Joshua 11:21-23)*.

INDEPENDENCE Day

A driver's license. Cash flow. College. Your own place. What teenager doesn't look forward to these milestones of independence?

The drive for independence is a natural stage of adolescence. Without it, teenagers would remain, well, teenagers. Healthy independence is a good thing.

Sometimes, though, teenagers get a skewed perspective of what it is to be independent. They get the notion that to prove their independence, they need to cut all ties with parents and families. They believe that they must reject their parents' values and religious convictions to demonstrate that they have their own lives.

Healthy independence doesn't mean breaking ties. Healthy independence means taking responsibility for your own choices. It's exciting when teenagers realize that independence can mean making a faith commitment of their own and when they stop counting on Mom and Dad's faith to carry them along.

Use this study to help teenagers discover that independence and responsibility go hand in hand and that the truly mature Christian is one who lives in healthy relationships with other people.

THE POINT

Independence from your family is a lifelong process.

SCRIPTURE SOURCE

Luke 16:10-12
Jesus explains that we must be faithful with what we are given.

1 Corinthians 13:11;
Ephesians 4:14-16, 25-32
Paul addresses mature and immature Christian behavior.

THE STUDY AT A GLANCE

#1

For Starters

15 to 20 minutes

■ **SYMBOLS OF INDEPENDENCE**

What students will do:
Choose and explain objects that represent independence for them.

SUPPLIES:
❑ various supplies

#2

Bible Truth

20 to 25 minutes

■ **CREATIVE MEMORIES**

What students will do:
Create pages in a photo album to demonstrate how they have matured.

SUPPLIES:
❑ Bibles
❑ magazines
❑ scissors
❑ tape
❑ markers
❑ pens
❑ paper

#3

Life Application

10 to 15 minutes

■ **GROWTH CHARTS**

What students will do:
Make "growth charts" to evaluate how mature their behavior is at home.

SUPPLIES:
❑ Bibles
❑ paper
❑ pens

■ **BONUS ACTIVITY**
5 to 10 minutes

What students will do:
Write a note of appreciation to a family member who has modeled maturity.

SUPPLIES:
❑ thank you cards
❑ envelopes
❑ pens

BEFORE THE STUDY

For the "Symbols of Independence" activity, gather a variety of supplies that can symbolize freedom and independence for teenagers. For example, you could collect car keys, a diploma, money, a Bible, a business card, a telephone, a charge card, a computer disk, sports equipment, and suntan lotion. Set the supplies in the middle of the room.

FOR STARTERS

15 to 20 minutes

SYMBOLS OF INDEPENDENCE

Have teenagers sit in a circle around the supplies you gathered before the study.

Say: I'm going to have you take turns finding something in this pile, something you've brought in, or something in this room that represents your definition of independence. For example, if independence for you is driving your own car, you could grab the car keys. Then tell the rest of the group how the object represents independence and how you feel about your current level of independence.

Have students take turns choosing an item, explaining how it represents independence, putting the item back, then telling the group how they feel about their current level of independence.

After all the students have had a turn, **ask:**

- Have you seen your level of independence change as you grow older?

- In what areas would you like more independence?

- What responsibilities aren't you ready to take on right now?

Say: One of the most exciting things about growing up is the opportunity for more independence. It can be frustrating when you feel that you don't have as much independence as you believe you're ready for. But independence from your family is a lifelong process. The best way to gain more independence is to act responsibly and respectfully with the privileges and independence you currently have. As you show yourself to be consistently trustworthy and mature, your family, teachers, coaches, and leaders will become more comfortable with giving you more independence and responsibility.

BIBLE TRUTH

20 to 25 minutes

CREATIVE MEMORIES

Set out magazines, scissors, tape, markers, and pens. Give each student a sheet of paper. **Say:**

On your sheet of paper, make a page in a scrapbook or photo album of your life. This page of your album should demonstrate what responsibility was like in your life from the time you were born to the age of ten. Use pictures from the magazines, draw pictures, or write words to demonstrate what you were able to do, what responsibilities you had, and what had to be done for you. You have only five minutes, so work quickly.

After five minutes, have students form groups of four to **discuss** these questions:

- Show your picture to the group. What does the page say about your independence as a child?

- As a child how would you have handled additional responsibilities such as holding down a job, paying the bills, or taking care of siblings?

- Read 1 Corinthians 13:11. How has the way you think and reason changed as you have grown up?

- What childish ways have you put behind you?

- What things did you want to do as a child that you may not have been ready for?

Give each student another sheet of paper. **Say:**

I'd like you to create another picture for your album. This time, demonstrate what responsibility is like in your life right now. Demonstrate what things you do and what things are done for you. Remember to work quickly.

After five minutes, have teenagers return to their groups to **discuss** these questions:

- Share your pictures with your group. How has your life changed for the better since you were a child? for the worse?

- How do you feel about your current level of responsibility?

- Read Ephesians 4:14-16. How have you grown up in Christ?

● Do you think you have too much or not enough independence and responsibility for your age? Explain.

● What mistakes have you made with the independence and responsibility you've already been given?

● What successes have you had?

● In what ways do you still need to grow up in Christ?

● What responsibilities do you wish you had?

● What responsibilities are you glad you don't have to deal with?

Direct teenagers to make one more page for their albums. This time, the page should reflect how they see their independence and responsibilities in five years. As a class **discuss** these questions:

● Are you looking forward to or dreading having more responsibility?

● Are you ready for it? Explain.

● Do you feel that you are spiritually mature? Why or why not?

Read Luke 16:10-12 aloud. **Say:**

Most of us, including adults, feel that we are ready for more independence and responsibility than we have. Sometimes we're right, but sometimes we're not ready for the responsibility we want. Independence from **THE POINT** your family is a lifelong process. You have much more independence today than you had when you were a child. And you'll have much more independence in five years. However, we need to take the Bible's direction to work on becoming mature and growing up right now. We do not have to have greater responsibilities to become mature; we just need to be wise, faithful, and mature with the responsibilities we currently have.

LIFE APPLICATION

10 to 15 minutes

GROWTH CHARTS

Form pairs. Give each person a sheet of paper and a pen.
Say: With your partner, read Ephesians 4:25-32. Then make a "growth chart" for yourself. Draw a line down the middle of your paper. On the left side, write down characteristics and habits a person must have to be considered mature. Use Ephesians 4:25-32 as a starting place.

Give pairs about five minutes to make their lists. **Say:**

On the right side of your paper, rank yourself on a scale of one to five for each of the characteristics and habits according to the way you live at home. One stands for "needs considerable improvement," and five stands for "very strong in this area."

After about five minutes, have pairs **discuss** these questions:

● Is it harder to be mature with your family or with your friends? Explain.

● If this growth chart reflects your maturity and level of independence, how happy are you with where you are?

● Why do you think this kind of growing up might be a lifelong process?

Have partners share an area in which they need to grow up and then pray for each other about those areas.

One of the characteristics of an adult, according to Ephesians 4:15, is that adults "speak the truth in love." Literally, that phrase could be translated "truthing" or "doing the truth." What does it mean to do the truth? Paul spells it out in the next part of the chapter. He tells us to put on the new self and to put off things like falsehood, stealing, unwholesome talk, and every form of malice.

In *The Expositor's Bible Commentary,* Bible scholar Frank E. Gaebelein points out that this passage teaches that "concern for the truth is the secret of maturity." Without responsible, truthful living, no one can claim to be mature.

FYI

We often use the words *freedom* and *independence* interchangeably. But in the Bible, *freedom* has a slightly different connotation. In the Old Testament, Israel's freedom from foreign oppression was always bound up with dependence on God. It was when Israel tried to become independent of God that she ended up in slavery to other nations. The books by the Old Testament prophets tell this story again and again.

In the New Testament, we read much about freedom from the Law and freedom from sin. But the way we receive this freedom is by becoming "slaves"—that is, devoting our entire allegiance and obedience—to Christ.

As you lead your students through this lesson, help them see that true freedom means total dependence on Jesus Christ.

>> BONUS ACTIVITY

To take the life application a step further, try this optional activity.

Give each student a thank you card and an envelope. Instruct teenagers to write thank you notes to someone in their families. Encourage teenagers to express appreciation for the way those people have modeled maturity and helped them grow in independence and responsibility. If teenagers have trouble thinking of something to write, suggest that they take a particular quality from the growth charts they made earlier.

Have teenagers seal their envelopes. Then **say:**

Independence from your family is a lifelong ◀THE POINT **process. One step in that process is recognizing and appreciating the positive things about your family. Be sure to give your note to the person you wrote it for so that person knows you appreciate him or her for helping you grow and become independent.**

If you'd rather not buy thank you cards for your students, give each teenager a sheet of paper and an envelope for his or her thank you card.

If you have time, have teenagers write thank you cards to each person in their families.

CHANGED 4 LIFE

To make sure the Bible truth in these studies penetrates your students' hearts and lives, try setting up family accountability relationships.

Recruit families in your church who are willing to participate in relationships to help them relate in healthy ways. Match interested families with one another, and instruct them to meet on a regular basis (once a month or so) and keep in touch with each other.

When partner families meet, they should discuss how their family relationships are functioning, how they're handling problems as a family, and how they're working to make their family relationships stronger.

Here are some suggested questions families can discuss with one another:

- **How are you getting along as family members?**

- **What are you struggling with as a family?**

- **How are you addressing challenges and struggles?**

- **How are you showing each other that you value your family?**

- **What are you doing to make your family stronger and healthier?**

Look for the Whole Family of **Faith 4 LiFE** Bible Studies!

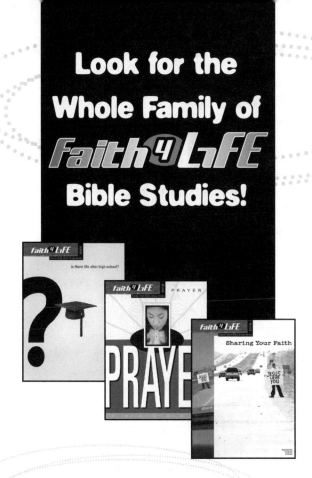

Senior High Books
- ■ *Family Matters*
- ■ *Is There Life After High School?*
- ■ *Prayer*
- ■ *Sharing Your Faith*

Junior High Books
- ■ *Becoming a Christian*
- ■ *Finding Your Identity*
- ■ *God's Purpose for Me*
- ■ *Understanding the Bible*

Preteen Books
- ■ *Being Responsible*
- ■ *Getting Along With Others*
- ■ *God in My Life*
- ■ *Going Through Tough Times*

Coming Soon!

for Senior High {
- ■ *Applying God's Word*
- ■ *Christian Character*
- ■ *Sexuality*
- ■ *Your Christian ID*
- ■ *Believing in Jesus*
- ■ *Following Jesus*
- ■ *Worshipping 24/7*
- ■ *Your Relationships*

for Junior High {
- ■ *Choosing Wisely*
- ■ *Friends*
- ■ *My Family Life*
- ■ *Sharing Jesus*
- ■ *Fighting Temptation*
- ■ *How to Pray*
- ■ *My Life as a Christian*
- ■ *Who Is God?*

for Preteens {
- ■ *Building Friendships*
- ■ *How to Make Great Choices*
- ■ *Succeeding in School*
- ■ *What's a Christian?*
- ■ *Handling Conflict*
- ■ *Peer Pressure*
- ■ *The Bible and Me*
- ■ *Why God Made Me*

Visit your local Christian bookstore,
or contact Group Publishing, Inc., at 800-447-1070.
www.grouppublishing.com

Dynamic Resources for Energizing Students' Faith

Go Deeper Retreats: 12 Life-Changing Weekends for Youth Ministry

In these 12 complete, high-impact retreats you'll dig deep into a Bible story or character and apply Bible truth to teen-interest topics through interaction and discussion. For example, study Jonah and discuss how to love the unlovely. Includes large group, small group and individual sessions and activities. Alternate 1-night lock-in plans for each retreat. Tons of extra ideas and tips to ensure an awesome retreat. Includes reproducible student quiet time handouts.

ISBN 0-7644-2358-4

Discovering Jesus: A Multimedia Journey

Experience Jesus Like Never Before!

Use *Discovering Jesus* to put together a dynamic, multimedia tour through Jesus' birth, death, and resurrection. As participants are led on this heart-gripping journey by a written guide and CD of worship and narratives by characters in the story, they will be inspired to draw closer to Jesus. They will experience God's Presence in a powerful, potentially life-changing way.

This can includes all of these creative tools for creating an unusual and compelling spiritual encounter experience in your church or community:

• Illustrated Leader Guide with complete, easy-to-follow instructions for creating a 10-station, self-guided worship adventure.

• 10 captivating, devotional guides to guide participants on their journey and to focus them on Christ and a relationship with him.

• 6 accompanying CDs that act as "audio guides" to the stations in the journey for up to six people at a time.

• 2 videos, *Water* and *Anna*, that enhance stations on the journey, engaging participants and emphasizing how personally meaningful the truths of Jesus' life, death, and resurrection are to each of us.

Use *Discovering Jesus* at your next church special event, retreat, camp, or innovative outreach event for your community. Get ready to discover...or *re-discover* Jesus!

ISBN 0-7644-2384-3

Additional CDs
6 CD set UPC 646847-12842-4
Single CD UPC 646847-12832-5

Additional Participant Guides
10 pack ISBN 0-7644-2420-3

The Winning Spirit: Empowering Teenagers Through God's Grace

Chris Hill

This youth ministry veteran details a fresh vision and practical philosophy for youth ministry. It's about loving kids as Jesus loves them. Grace-based youth ministry that gives students a God's-eye view of themselves, as winners. In this book, you'll find...

• a new perspective on youth ministry that transforms students' lives through love and grace, set against a backdrop of the biblical story of David—before Goliath

• a strong foundation for life-changing ministry along with a lot of practical ideas and examples from the author's ministry

• real-life accounts of young people's lives changed through love and grace

Be inspired, encouraged, and motivated by a new dream for your youth ministry.

ISBN 0-7644-2396-7

Chris Hill is an 18-year youth ministry veteran of successful grace-based youth ministry in both urban and suburban settings. A sought-after speaker and writer, he currently serves as youth pastor for The Potter's House in Dallas, Texas, where Bishop T.D. Jakes serves as pastor—the largest African-American church in the country.

Searching for the Truth: How Christianity Compares to World Religions (Kit)

These 6 easy-to-prepare lessons will help students better understand and grow in their Christian faith as compared to other world religions and cults. The student booklets provide summary information on Christianity and other belief systems and religions, providing teenagers with a handy, keepable resource they can refer to in the future and use to confidently help friends better understand Christianity. Satisfy your teens' curiosity about other religions, while engaging their hearts with the truth of Christianity.

ISBN 0-7644-2393-2
(Kit contents: Leader Guide and 10 Student Booklets)

Additional Student Books
5 pack ISBN 0-7644-2394-0